Your *Bettermind* Journal

A daily guide to reaching your mind's full potential.

"What we think, we become."
-Buddha

Our Promise

Welcome to Your Bettermind Journal, an innovative guide that will show you how to place yourself in a positive mindset, manage your focus, and push your abilities to the limit.

The methods used in this journal are inspired by Neuroscience, the study of the structure and function of the brain and nervous system, as well as real world experience. It's our goal to share these science based exercises with as many individuals as possible so we can all move closer to the goal of achieving maximum potential.

One of the most effective ways to develop a new skill is through repetition, so we've packed this journal with habit forming activities that will teach you to control your focus and ultimately transform the way you think, feel and perform.

How do you know if you're tapping into your full creativity? How do you know if you're doing your best work and reaching your full potential? It all comes down to achieving focused concentration of attention or energy on what is important to you.

Your Bettermind Journal is designed to introduce you to powerful insights learned through Neuroscience so you can effectively apply these principles in your everyday life.

Three Principles

to achieving your *Bettermind.*

Principle

№ 1

Journaling

Getting into the habit of writing down your observations in a journal can help you practice noticing. What is "noticing"? It's really just being more aware of your thoughts, emotions, and actions. But developing that awareness opens the door to managing your attention span, which is the key to improving, and ultimately mastering your focus.

As you start journaling, you'll find yourself gradually feeling more present. It doesn't take much. Just a short entry daily or every other day, can make a big difference in your life. Expressing yourself creatively, as you do when you write in a journal, is a powerful tool for relieving stress and enabling you to recognize the things in life that aren't serving you.

Journaling regularly will help you organize your thoughts, express yourself more effectively, and process your emotions (both positive and negative) more constructively. This is an important first step on the way to achieving a positive mindset, improved focus and ultimately a happier, healthier mind.

Principle
№ 2

Positive Mindset

Mindset is everything, especially when you want to achieve your best work. ***The 4 PILLARS of a Positive Mindset*** will transform your way of thinking and train your mind to reduce anxiety and help you feel happier overall.

1. Gratitude - By practicing a regular habit of gratitude, you will begin to see and think differently.

2. Label Emotions - You feel awful today. Give that feeling a name. Sad? Anxious? Angry? Simply describing an emotion in just a word or two helps to put things into perspective.

3. Decide - Make that decision. Neuroscience suggests the act of decision making reduces worry and anxiety, and encourages you to take action. Making a "good enough" decision is enough.

4. Touch - We need to feel love and acceptance from others and when we do not, it's painful. Relationships are very important to your feelings and happiness. Take it to the next level by hugging or holding someone's hand. Even handshakes or pats on the back make a difference.

Principle

№ 3

Attention Span & Focus

If you want to achieve maximum potential, you must learn to sustain your attention. When practiced regularly, ***The 5 RULES of Attention Span & Focus*** will significantly increase your patience and allow you to think more clearly and concisely.

1. Stop Multitasking - Multitasking reduces your efficiency and performance because your brain can only truly focus on one thing at a time. When you try to do two things at once, your brain lacks the capacity to perform both tasks successfully.

2. Exercise - Exercise improves blood flow and memory; it stimulates chemical changes in the brain that enhance learning, mood and thinking.

3. Meditate - Studies show that meditation helps relieve our subjective levels of anxiety and depression and improve attention, concentration and overall psychological well-being.

4. Mother Nature - Nature gives us a physical and mental sense of being away from our busy, everyday lives. Whether images or the real deal, nature scenes give us visually-rich stimuli that nourish the brain.

5. Reduce Interference - Creating a distraction free environment when trying to complete your best work is critically important. Learning to "batch" check email, texting and social media are good examples of creating a distraction free environment.

A few things to note

before you start your journey.

Knowing Where You Are

At the start of each section, the left side of Your Bettermind Journal shows which of the three principles you are working on, along with an inspirational quote that pertains to that section.

On the right side of the page, you will see the supporting parts of the principle you are working on, for example, ***The 5 RULES of Attention Span & Focus*** as shown below. You'll know exactly the type of skills you're developing and where you are in the process.

5 RULES

1. **STOP MULTITASKING**
2. EXERCISE
3. MEDITATE
4. MOTHER NATURE
5. REDUCE INTERFERENCE

Degree of Difficulty

Your Bettermind Journal is marked with a visual aid on the lower left side of each section. It tells you the degree of difficulty for each exercise and how much effort is required to complete an exercise. Work your way through the various activities and graduate to expert level.

Never Feel Behind

Your Bettermind Journal is designed to be flexible and friendly to use. If you go on vacation or take time off, you can pick up where you left off without having to skip any sections. You don't even have to go in order. Feel free to skip around depending on how you're feeling that day. Just write in the date and circle the day of the week as you go.

DATE **7-21**

S M Ⓣ W T F S

It's time to begin

your journey to achieving a *Bettermind*.

№ 1

Journaling is paying attention to the inside for the purpose of living well from the inside out.

-Lee Wise

Journaling

 **STARTING OUT SMALL**

Try stream of consciousness journaling. Write about everything and nothing as a non-judgmental flow of your thoughts. This is a simple way of training your brain to release thoughts through the pen and onto paper.

FREEDOM SPACE

NOTE - *Use the free space above to sketch and doodle all the random thoughts in your head. It will help you concentrate and spur creative insight.*

Journaling *continued*

Journaling *continued*

If you want to find happiness, find gratitude.

-Steve Maraboli

Positive Mindset

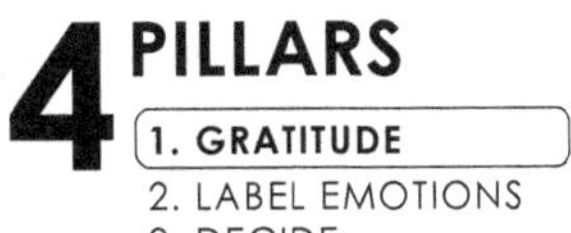

☺ GRATITUDE

Write down one thing you are grateful for.

....

....

NOTE - *Ask "What am I grateful for?" No answers? It doesn't matter. Just searching makes you feel better.*

◎ CHALLENGE

Describe a time when your positive attitude influenced someone you care about.

....

....

....

....

....

....

....

NOTE - *Gratitude doesn't just make you feel better. It can also create a positive feedback loop in your relationships.*

Principle
№ 2

Labeling your emotions is key. If you can name it, you can tame it.

-Marc Brackett

Positive Mindset

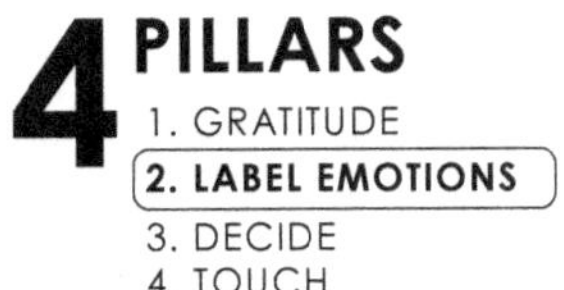

✏️ LABELING

Describe in just one or two words a negative emotion you sometimes feel.

....

....

NOTE - *Not feeling great? Just give that feeling a name. Sad? Anxious? Angry? It's that simple. You are on your way to feeling better.*

◉ CHALLENGE

When a loved one asks "How was your day?", try being as honest and descriptive as possible in your response.

☐
Completed

NOTE - *It's difficult for many of us to authentically share and articulate how we feel. As a result, we may struggle to feel comfortable sharing our feelings with others.*

Principle
№ 2

You cannot make progress without making decisions.

-Jim Rohn

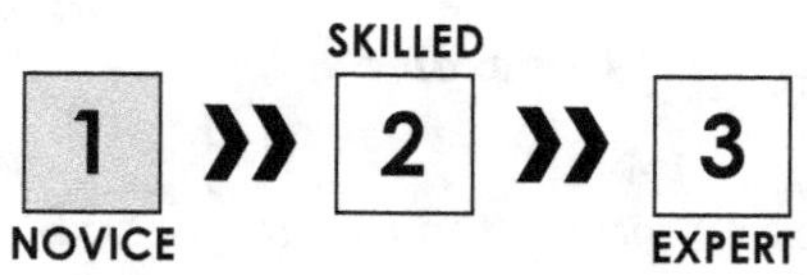

Positive Mindset

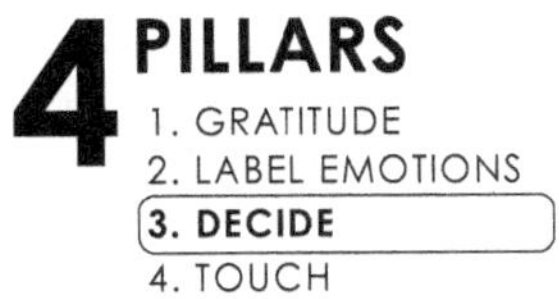

? DECIDE

Make a "good enough" decision and write it down below. It doesn't have to be the best decision you've ever made.

....

....

....

....

....

....

NOTE - *Your mind feels you have more control when you make a decision. A feeling of control reduces stress and boosts pleasure.*

⊙ CHALLENGE

Follow through with the decision you made above.

☐
Completed

NOTE - *Trying to be a perfectionist can be stressful. It can make you feel out of control and may stimulate negative emotions.*

Principle
№ 2

Nothing eases suffering like human touch.

-Bobby Fischer

Positive Mindset

✋ TOUCH

The next time you hug someone, apply a little more pressure than usual. Write down how you feel afterwards.

....

....

....

NOTE - *Holding hands, hugging, cuddling, they're all pretty effective. What we find is that when you apply more pressure, moderate pressure, as in a hug or giving a person a back rub, the effects are more positive than using less pressure.*

◎ CHALLENGE

Give someone a back or foot rub to someone who's deserving.

☐

Completed

NOTE - *Did you know that fast walking can be a form of self massage? When you're walking, you're increasing serotonin and stimulating the pressure sensors in your feet.*

№1

Gratitude opens the door to the power, the wisdom, the creativity of the universe. You open the door through gratitude.

-Deepak Chopra

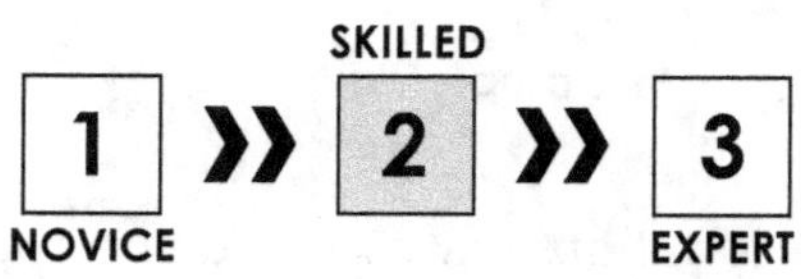

Journaling

✏️ SEEK POSITIVITY

Studies show the human brain is wired to prioritize negativity. This trait was important to help us avoid serious threats when survival was more difficult for humans. Nowadays, the stresses we experience are more social than physical and rarely pose a threat to our survival. Focusing on the things, events and people we are grateful for can help put social stresses in perspective and counter the natural emphasis on negativity. Look for ways to seek out and prioritize positivity in your life and write some examples below.

NOTE - *Use the free space above to sketch and doodle all the random thoughts in your head. It will help you concentrate and spur creative insight.*

Journaling *continued*

Journaling *continued*

Principle
№ 3

Multitasking arises out of distraction itself.

-Marilyn vos Savant

Attention Span & Focus

5 RULES

1. **STOP MULTITASKING**
2. EXERCISE
3. MEDITATE
4. MOTHER NATURE
5. REDUCE INTERFERENCE

◎ CHALLENGE

Try not to look at your phone for the first 30 minutes of the morning.

☐

Completed

NOTE - *Checking your phone right after you wake will put you in a reactive state of mind.*

📝 PRIORITIZE

What are the two most important things you want to achieve today? Learn to list out priorities daily.

1 ....

....

2 ....

....

NOTE - *Don't try to do important work while checking email, texting and posting on social media.*

Walking brings me back to myself.

-Laurette Mortimer

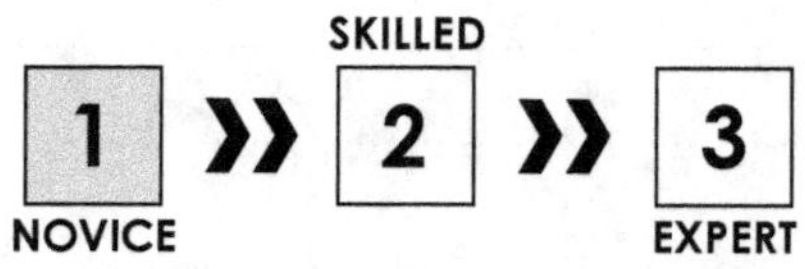

Attention Span & Focus

5 RULES

1. STOP MULTITASKING
2. **EXERCISE**
3. MEDITATE
4. MOTHER NATURE
5. REDUCE INTERFERENCE

◉ CHALLENGE

It's time to move during your lunch hour. Try taking just 10 minutes for a physical activity like speed walking.

☐

Completed

NOTE - *10 minutes of cardio increases your heart rate, blood circulation and burns calories. It's also good for your mental health.*

✛ DAILY WORKOUT

No equipment necessary.

☐ 25 Jumping Jacks

☐ 15 Squats

☐ 5 Pushups

NOTE - *Mark that check box with pride! Tracking your workout progress provides accountability and a sense of accomplishment.*

Principle
№ 3

Quiet the mind, and the soul will speak.

-Ma Jaya Sati Bhagavati

SKILLED

| 1 | » | 2 | » | 3 |

NOVICE · EXPERT

Attention Span & Focus

5 RULES

1. STOP MULTITASKING
2. EXERCISE
3. **MEDITATE**
4. MOTHER NATURE
5. REDUCE INTERFERENCE

🪨 MEDITATION BASICS

1. Sit or lie comfortably.

2. Close your eyes.

3. Make no effort to control your breath, just breathe naturally.

4. Focus your attention on the breath and how the body moves with each inhalation and exhalation. Notice the movement of your body as you breathe.

NOTE - *Maintain this meditation practice for two to three minutes to start, then gradually work towards longer periods.*

◎ CHALLENGE

Using the above steps, meditate for 3 days in a row.

☐	☐	☐
Day 1	**Day 2**	**Day 3**

NOTE - *Meditation causes shifts in our awareness. Many people over identify with their thoughts and emotions, which can prolong them and make them feel bigger than they are. Specific thoughts or feelings can agonize us for days on end.*

№ 3

Our very being, essence, health and happiness depend on Mother Earth.

-David Suzuki

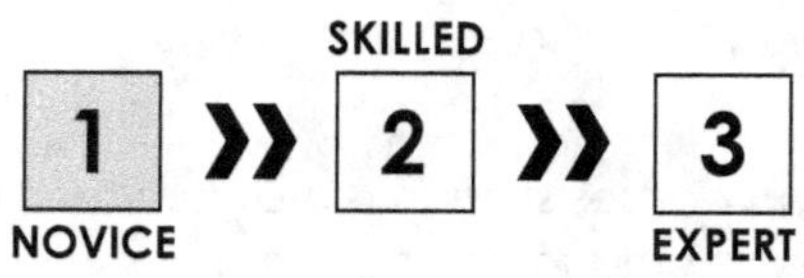

Attention Span & Focus

5 RULES

1. STOP MULTITASKING
2. EXERCISE
3. MEDITATE
4. **MOTHER NATURE**
5. REDUCE INTERFERENCE

◎ CHALLENGE

Feel the earth beneath your feet. Stand barefoot on grass and focus on your connection to the earth.

☐

Completed

NOTE - Close your eyes and notice how solid the ground feels beneath your feet.

📝 MAKE A LIST

Go outside, close your eyes and listen to nature. Make a list of the things you hear.

....

....

....

....

NOTE - Open all your senses. Hear, see, smell, taste, and feel. You will be surprised at how much you notice that wasn't apparent before.

Principle
№ 3

Work is hard. Distractions are plentiful. And time is short.

-Adam Hochschild

Attention Span & Focus

5 RULES

1. STOP MULTITASKING
2. EXERCISE
3. MEDITATE
4. MOTHER NATURE
5. **REDUCE INTERFERENCE**

⊙ CHALLENGE

Before you start work, get comfortable. Think about the clothes you're wearing, your chair, the sounds in the background, the temperature of the room.

☐

Completed

NOTE - *Knowing what environment makes you comfortable can help you maintain focus through the work day.*

📝 MAKE A LIST

Turn off notifications for at least three phone apps and list them below.

1 ....

2 ....

3 ....

NOTE - *Controlling your devices, and not having that technology control you, may help reduce distractions and increase your focus.*

Principle
№1

It's not hard to write when your hand is led by your heart.

-Sissy Gavrilaki

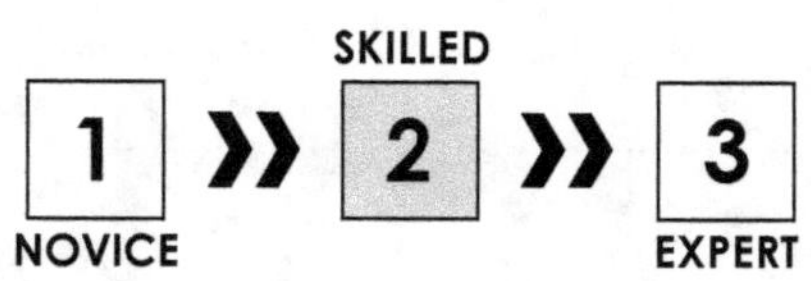

Journaling

 **THOUGHTS, FEELINGS & EMOTIONS**

In this complex society, our minds can be dominated by worries and stress. This can occupy valuable mind-space and limit your capacity for generating ideas and problem solving. Write down your most dominant thoughts and feelings at the moment to get them out of your head and onto paper.

NOTE - *Use the free space above to sketch and doodle all the random thoughts in your head. It will help you concentrate and spur creative insight.*

Principle
№ 2

*If we believe that tomorrow will be better,
we can bear a hardship today.*

-Thich Nhat Hanh

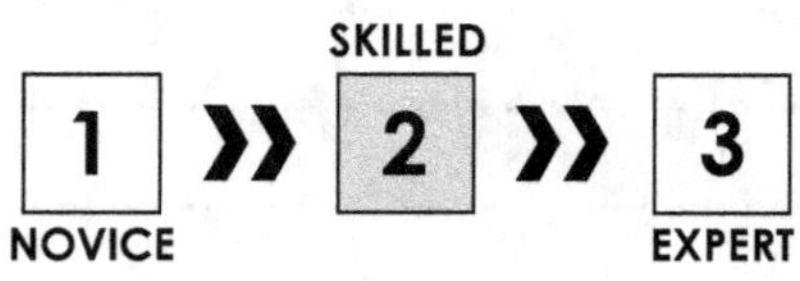

Positive Mindset

4 PILLARS

1. **GRATITUDE**
2. LABEL EMOTIONS
3. DECIDE
4. TOUCH

☺ REMEMBER THE BAD

To be grateful in your current state, it's helpful to remember the hard times that you once experienced. Describe a difficult time in the past and think about how you overcame it and where you are now.

....

....

....

....

....

....

....

....

....

....

....

NOTE - *When you remember how difficult life used to be and how far you've come, you set up an explicit contrast in your mind. This contrast is fertile ground for gratefulness.*

Principle
N⚬ 2

Emotion can be the enemy, if you give into your emotion, you lose yourself. You must be at one with your emotions, because the body always follows the mind.

-Bruce Lee

Positive Mindset

ACTIVITY

When you feel upset, try filling in the blanks below.

- My body is telling me I'm ....

(Deep Breath)

- I'm having thoughts that this is ....

(Deep Breath)

- I'm feeling ....

NOTE - *You may have noticed a distance that develops as you label your thoughts and emotions after the initial event. Instead of lashing out or shutting down, slow your body and mind, and reflect on how you want to respond.*

CHALLENGE

Try to call out negative emotions on the fly without writing them down. It will take some practice, but you can make it a habit.

☐

Completed

NOTE - *If you can label your emotions as soon as you notice how you're feeling, managing them will become easier.*

*Your impact on the lives of others, your family,
the people at your church, your workmates, is
cultivated with each decision you make,
no matter how small.*

-Jim George

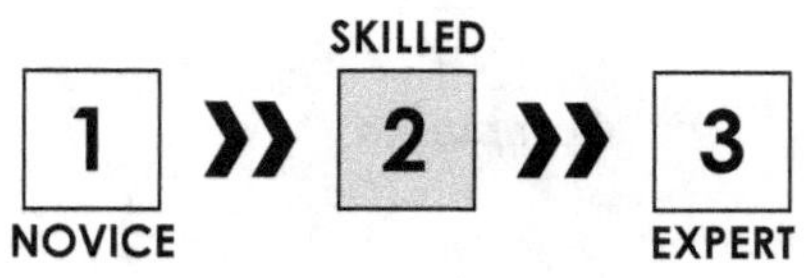

Positive Mindset

THINK ABOUT OTHERS BEFORE YOU DECIDE

If you think someone will have a negative response to an important decision you face, think through the possible reactions and write them down below. Putting yourself in the shoes of those impacted by your decision can help you find a good way to manage the situation.

....

....

....

....

....

....

....

....

....

....

NOTE - *When faced with a tough decision it's common to feel overwhelmed, anxious, wound up, pressured, confused, distracted and tired. Remember to take some time to relax or do something you enjoy.*

Principle
№2

Touch comes before sight, before speech. It is the first language, and the last, and it always tells the truth.

-Margaret Atwood

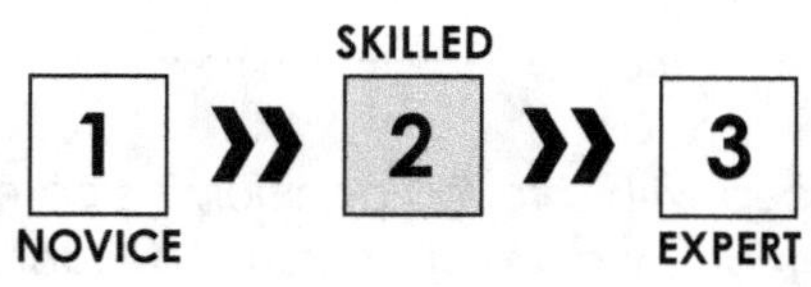

Positive Mindset

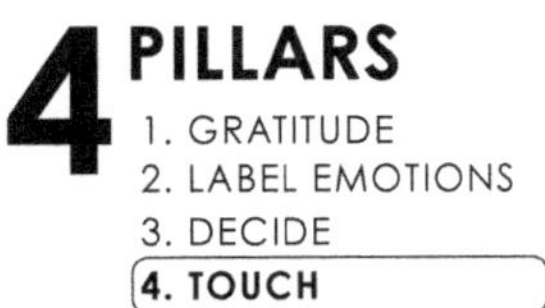

✋ TOUCH STARVED? START NOTICING

You may subconsciously do things to simulate touch, such as taking long, hot baths or showers, wrapping up in blankets, and holding a pet. Think back to a time when you may have subconsciously tried to simulate human touch and write it down below. How were you feeling during that time?

....

....

....

....

....

....

....

....

....

....

NOTE - *Touch calms our nervous center and slows down our heart beat. Touch also lowers blood pressure and cortisol, our stress hormone. It also triggers the release of oxytocin, a hormone known for promoting emotional bonding to others.*

№ 1

I write because I don't know what I think until I read what I say.

-Flannery O'Connor

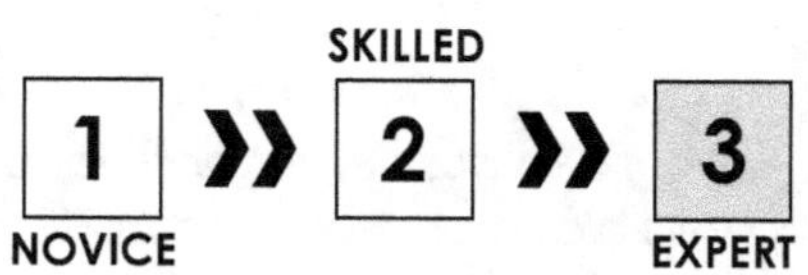

Journaling

✏️ BEGIN WITH THE END IN MIND

Know where you're going so you know what steps to take. Start by defining a goal you want to achieve. For example, clean the garage. Next, list all the smaller tasks required to achieve that goal with as much detail as possible. Determine if the order in which you complete the tasks is important. Then, jump into action.

NOTE - *Use the free space above to sketch and doodle all the random thoughts in your head. It will help you concentrate and spur creative insight.*

Journaling *continued*

Principle
№ 3

Your life is controlled by what you focus on.

-Tony Robbins

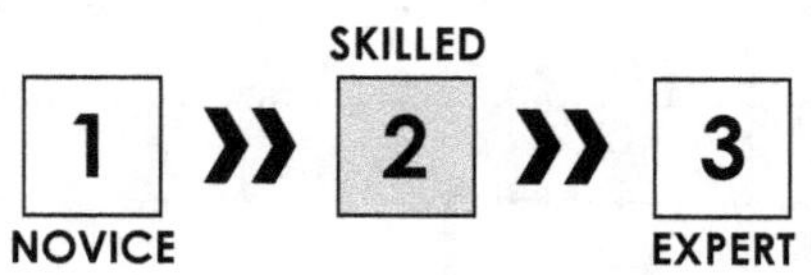

Attention Span & Focus

5 RULES

1. STOP MULTITASKING
2. EXERCISE
3. MEDITATE
4. MOTHER NATURE
5. REDUCE INTERFERENCE

VISUAL REMINDERS

Add two visual reminders, like a post it note, where you work and write down what they say in the spaces below. For example, *"Focus, Focus, Focus."* Be creative and make it look pretty. It's something you'll view often.

1 ....

2 ....

NOTE - *If you have difficulty sticking to a task or want to escape doing it to check email or social media, look at your visual reminders and repeat those words out loud.*

LEARN TO SAY NO

You don't have to be rude, just let them know you need more time before deciding. Try using the examples below so you can get back to your important work.

- *Let me think about it.*

- *Can I let you know later?*

NOTE - *Saying "no" allows you to choose where you put your energy. It allows you to focus on your most important goals, and the people, and parts of your life that deserve it most.*

Principle
№ 3

I may not be there yet, but I am closer than I was yesterday. Each step makes a difference.

-Liz Davidson

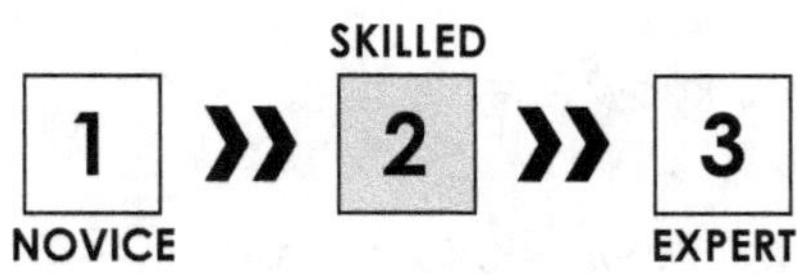

Attention Span & Focus

5 RULES

1. STOP MULTITASKING
2. **EXERCISE**
3. MEDITATE
4. MOTHER NATURE
5. REDUCE INTERFERENCE

◉ CHALLENGE

Instead of using an elevator or escalator, look for opportunities to take the stairs.

☐
Completed

NOTE - *Taking the stairs is great for working the major muscle groups in the legs and glutes. It will also provide more oxygen to the brain.*

✛ DAILY WORKOUT

No equipment necessary.

☐ 50 Jumping Jacks

☐ 30 Squats

☐ 10 Pushups

NOTE - *Tracking your workout progress provides accountability and a sense of accomplishment.*

*The thing about meditation is,
you become more and more you.*

-David Lynch

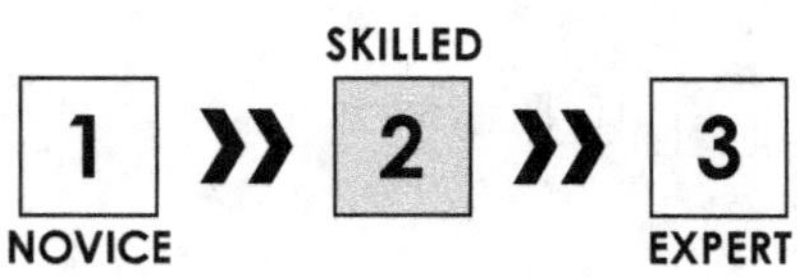

Attention Span & Focus

5 RULES

1. STOP MULTITASKING
2. EXERCISE
3. **MEDITATE**
4. MOTHER NATURE
5. REDUCE INTERFERENCE

🪨 LISTEN TO ONE SONG

Try to hear every instrument and separate the lyrics from the melody. Write down what you heard.

....

....

....

....

....

....

....

NOTE - *We often treat music like background noise, especially when working or performing other tasks. Listening to music all by itself is a good introduction to meditation.*

💡 TIPS BEFORE YOU MEDITATE

- *Start in the morning*
- *Same time, same place*
- *Get creative about location*
- *Don't sit cross-legged (if you don't think it's comfortable)*
- *Find the best position for you*

*Those who contemplate the beauty of the earth
find reserves of strength that will endure
as long as life lasts.*

-Rachel Carson

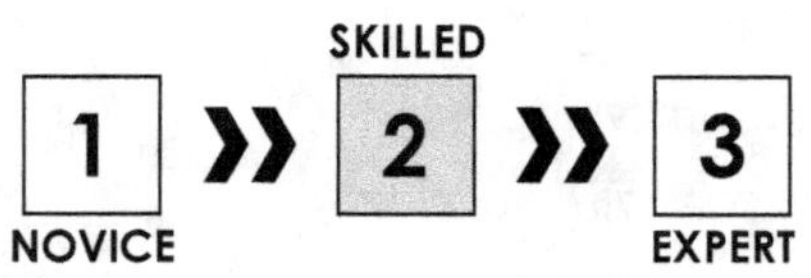

Attention Span & Focus

5 RULES

1. STOP MULTITASKING
2. EXERCISE
3. MEDITATE
4. **MOTHER NATURE**
5. REDUCE INTERFERENCE

MAKE A LIST

Write down the lowest priority or time-wasting things you do every day. Some examples are steaming TV, social media, and video games.

1 ....

2 ....

3 ....

CHALLENGE

Take just 10 minutes away from those low priority activities listed above and replace the time with being in nature.

Completed

NOTE - *Make nature more of a priority! If you're doing these low priority things, but you can't find 10 minutes to get outside and do something you love, that means you're not prioritizing being outside.*

Principle
№ 3

Distraction wastes our energy,
concentration restores it.

-Sharon Salzberg

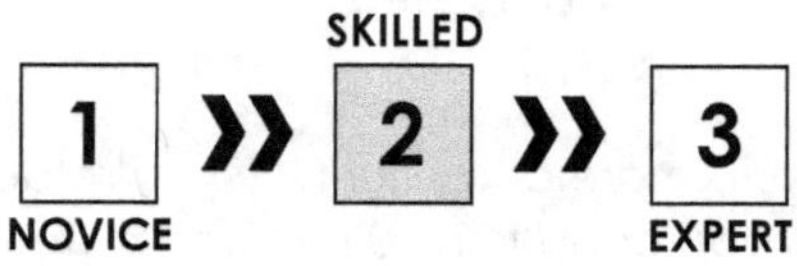

Attention Span & Focus

5 RULES

1. STOP MULTITASKING
2. EXERCISE
3. MEDITATE
4. MOTHER NATURE
5. REDUCE INTERFERENCE

◎ CHALLENGE

When you are ready to perform 'deep work', follow the steps below and mark when completed.

- Make it clear to yourself and others that you don't want to be distracted

- Turn off computer notifications

- Turn your phone off when you're not using it

- Schedule multiple breaks

Completed

NOTE - *To achieve deep work means to spend uninterrupted time with complete focus on the task at hand. You'll have to block out time for your priorities. This means turning off notifications and making yourself unavailable.*

Journal writing is a voyage to the interior.

-Christina Baldwin

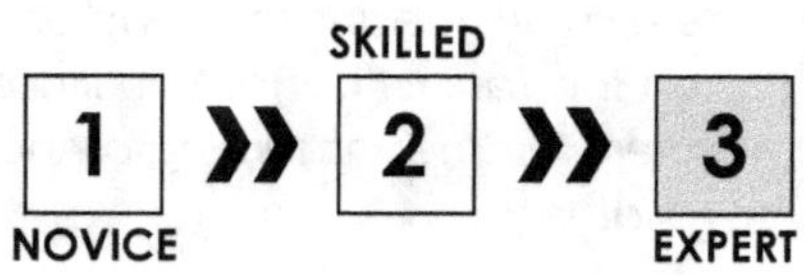

Journaling

✏️ USING YOUR FIVE SENSES

Describe your current surroundings and emotional state in detail and pay attention to all five senses. It's a way to get out of your own head and connect to the present moment.

NOTE - *Use the free space above to sketch and doodle all the random thoughts in your head. It will help you concentrate and spur creative insight.*

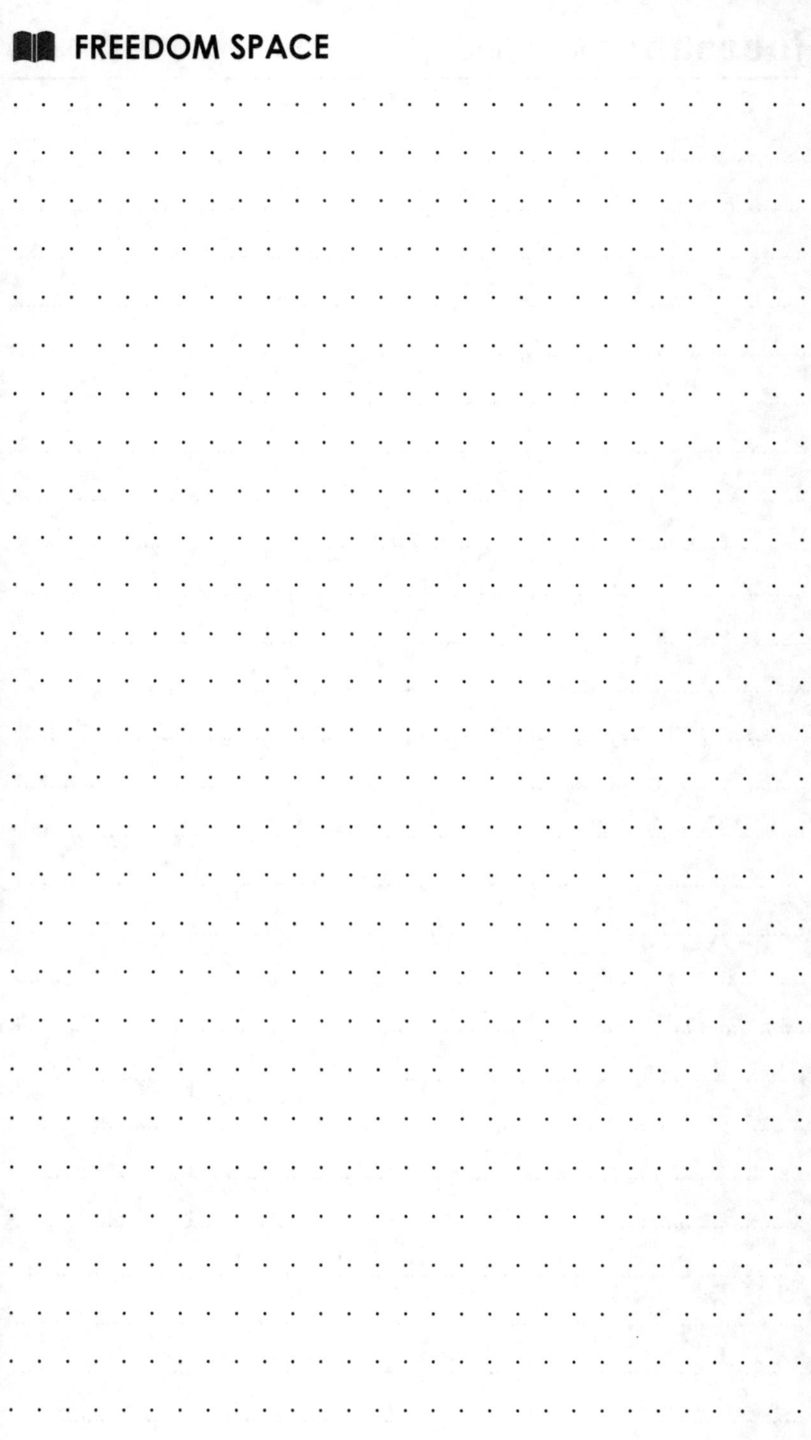

Journaling *continued*

Principle
№ 2

Gratitude unlocks the fullness of life. It turns what we have into enough and more.

-Melody Beattie

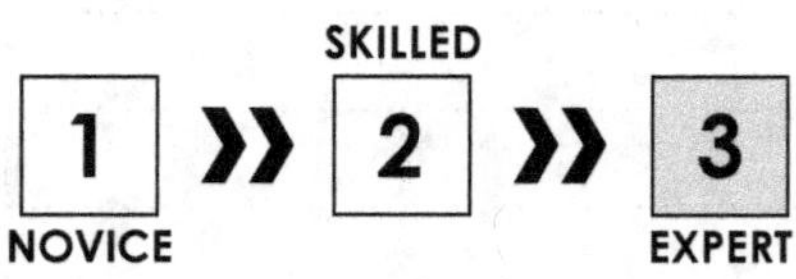

Positive Mindset

4 PILLARS

1. **GRATITUDE**
2. LABEL EMOTIONS
3. DECIDE
4. TOUCH

😊 CHANGE YOUR PERSPECTIVE

Put yourself in the shoes of someone who is experiencing misfortunes greater than your own and write it down below.

....

....

Write down something from yesterday that made you laugh.

....

....

NOTE - *Gratitude doesn't have to be saved for the "big" things in life. The habit of being grateful starts with appreciating the simple things.*

◉ CHALLENGE

Start a family gratitude journal and follow the steps below. You can use the free space provided in the back of this book or a blank notebook.

- Every night, ask family members what they are grateful for

- Write down and date each response

Completed

№2

Telling the story, acknowledging what has happened and how you feel, is often a necessary part of forgiveness.

-Sharon Salzberg

Positive Mindset

▲ ACTIVITY

We either acknowledge our emotions and call them out or we suppress and ignore them. Use the tips below to notice how you react to different emotional states throughout the day. Write down what you've learned on the next page.

-Acknowledge

- When I want to feel more positive emotion (such as joy or amusement), I change what I'm thinking about

- When I want to feel less negative emotion (such as sadness or anger), I change what I'm thinking about

- When I'm faced with a stressful situation, I make myself think about it in a way that helps me stay calm

-Suppress

- I keep my emotions to myself

- I control my emotions by not expressing them

- When I feel negative emotions, I try not to express them

NOTE - *It's important to recognize that negative or painful emotions are not inherently bad. You must accept that you will experience negative emotions in your life, no matter how happy or well balanced you may be.*

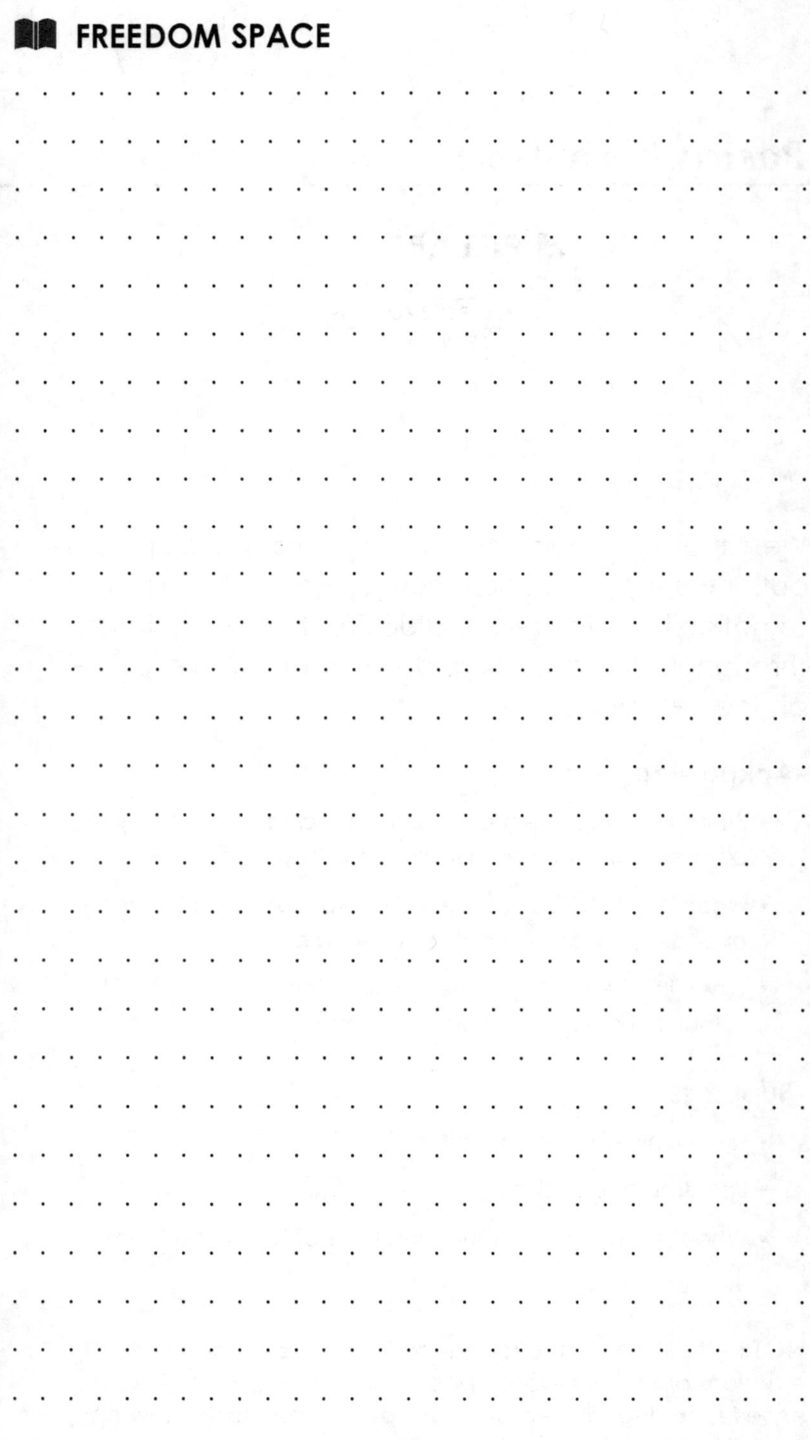

FREEDOM SPACE

Principle
№ 2

Always make decisions that prioritize your inner peace.

-Izey Victoria Odiase

Positive Mindset

♀ MAKING BETTER DECISIONS

If you educate yourself and make an effort to learn as much as you can about the situation, you will find the power within yourself to be decisive. When faced with a big decision, ask yourself the questions below and write down your best response.

- How important is this decision to me?

....

....

....

....

- When do I need to make this decision?

....

....

....

....

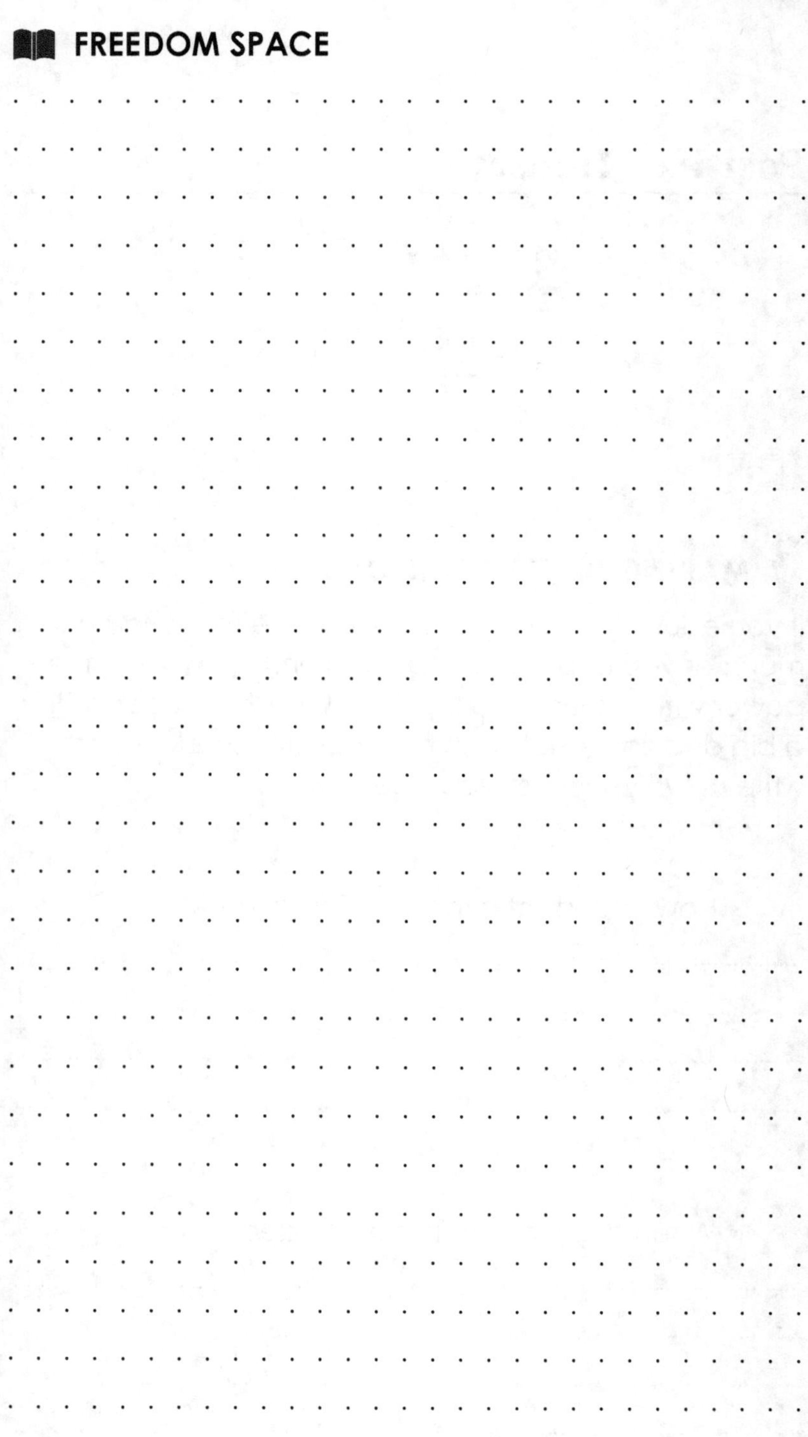

FREEDOM SPACE

Positive Mindset *continued*

- Name all the people that will be impacted.

- Who should I include in the decision-making process?

- Am I over-analyzing the situation?

NOTE - *The worst thing you can do when faced with a decision is to over-analyze the issue. Over-analyzing the situation will only make the decision seem more overwhelming. When faced with indecision, keep in mind that most bad decisions can be remedied and nothing is permanent.*

Principle
№ 2

*Your hand touching mine, this is
how galaxies collide.*

-Sanober Khan

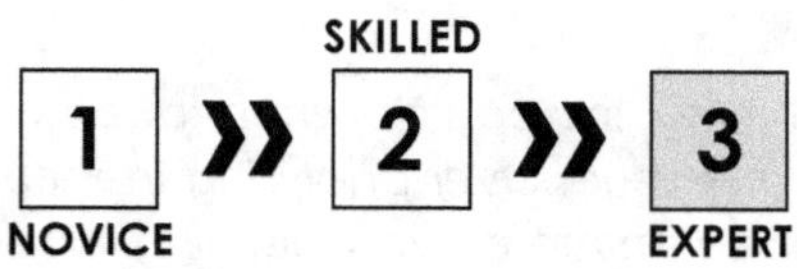

Positive Mindset

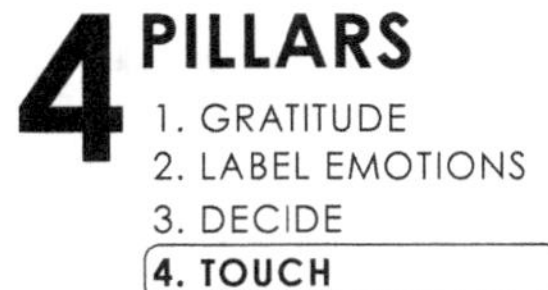

✋ COMMUNICATION WITHOUT WORDS

We can communicate emotion through touch, not just with those we are familiar with, but also with strangers. When appropriate, look for a time when someone is in need of companionship and use touch instead of words. Pay attention to how they react and write about the experience below.

....

....

....

....

....

....

....

....

....

NOTE - *Sometimes there are no words, but there is touch. Touch activates the body's vagus nerve which is intimately connected with our compassionate response. The vagus nerve is the pair of nerves that extends from the brain to the belly and passes the heart along the way.*

If I get lost, this journal will be like a record of who I was, a trail of bread crumbs to find my way back.

-Jonathan Tropper

Journaling

 **DESCRIBE YOURSELF TO A STRANGER**

If you were going to explain who you are to a stranger, how would that go? What are your likes, your dislikes, your strengths or weaknesses? Writing this prompt can go a long way in helping you identify how you think of yourself.

....

....

....

....

....

....

....

....

....

....

....

....

Journaling..

....

....

....

NOTE - *Use the free space above to sketch and doodle all the random thoughts in your head. It will help you concentrate and spur creative insight.*

Journaling *continued*

Journaling *continued*

Journaling *continued*

Principle
№ 3

If a goal is worth having, it is worth blocking out the time in your day-to-day life necessary to achieve it.

-Jill Koenig

Attention Span & Focus

5 RULES
1. **STOP MULTITASKING**
2. EXERCISE
3. MEDITATE
4. MOTHER NATURE
5. REDUCE INTERFERENCE

📝 SCHEDULE DAY IN HOUR BLOCKS

Think about what you need to accomplish today and break out the tasks in hour-long blocks. Write down what you plan to accomplish each hour of the work day. Set a timer each hour so you know when to switch to the next task. Feel free to add tasks like eat lunch, check emails or text messages, meditate, or pick up kids from school.

Time (hour 1): ________________

....

....

Time (hour 2): ________________

....

....

Time (hour 3): ________________

....

....

Time (hour 4): ________________

....

....

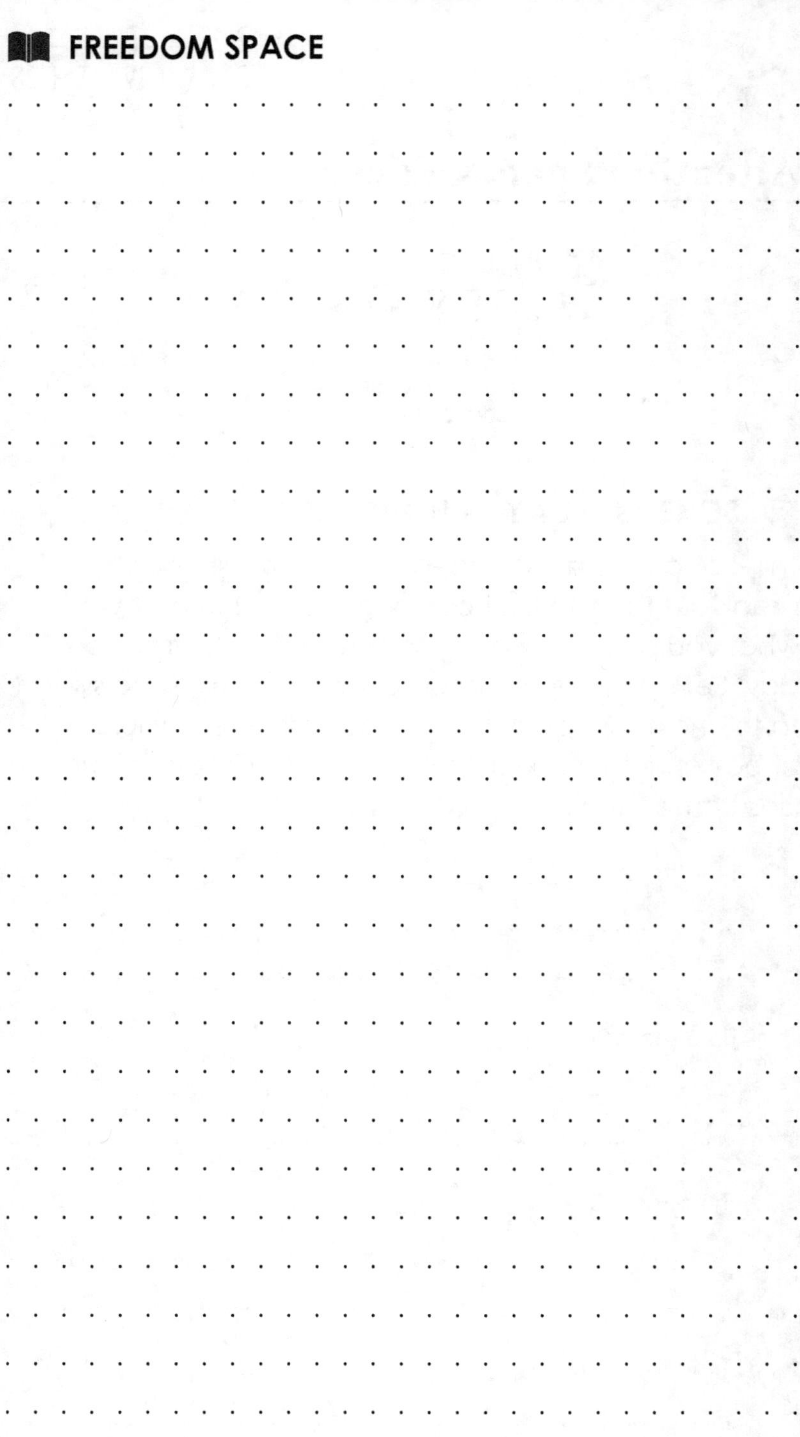

Attention Span & Focus *continued*

Time (hour 5): ______________

....

....

Time (hour 6): ______________

....

....

Time (hour 7): ______________

....

....

Time (hour 8): ______________

....

....

NOTE - *By scheduling every hour of your work day, you guard against distraction and increase productivity. When focusing on one task at a time, you can be up to 80% more productive than splitting your attention across multiple tasks.*

◊ TRY DIFFERENT TECHNIQUES

Try *The Pomodoro Technique*. Created in the 1980s by Francesco Cirillo as a time management strategy designed for sustaining energy and attention.

- **SET A TIMER FOR 25 MINUTES** - During this time, focus all of your attention and energy on completing the task at hand.

- **TAKE A SHORT BREAK WHEN YOU'RE DONE** - Use the break to rest your brain, body and attention. You can take a walk, have a cup of coffee or just rest your eyes for a few minutes.

- **EVERY FOUR ROUNDS, TAKE A LONGER BREAK** - About 30 minutes of dedicated rest time can help your cortisol levels reset and help you sustain your attention longer when you return to your next set of tasks.

Principle
№ 3

*To enjoy the glow of good health,
you must exercise.*

-Gene Tunney

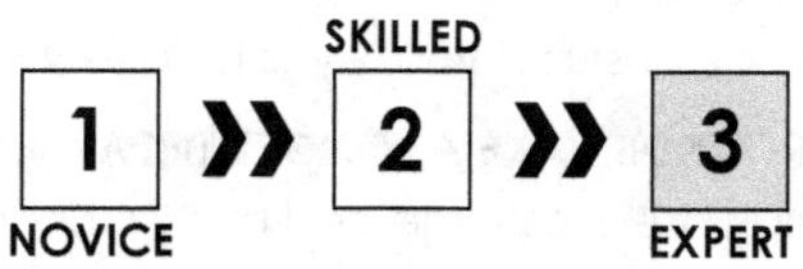

Attention Span & Focus

5 RULES

1. STOP MULTITASKING
2. **EXERCISE**
3. MEDITATE
4. MOTHER NATURE
5. REDUCE INTERFERENCE

◉ CHALLENGE

Try the *10-Minute Cardio Blast*. Warm up with a light jog in place (30 seconds), then complete the following five exercises:

- [ ] 30 seconds, **Jumping Jacks**, Rest 30 seconds

- [ ] 30 seconds, **Burpees**, Rest 30 seconds

- [ ] 30 seconds, **High Knees**, Rest 30 seconds

- [ ] 30 seconds, **Squat Jumps**, Rest 30 seconds

- [ ] 30 seconds, **Push-ups**, Rest 30 seconds

*Once you complete one round of all five exercises, rest for 60 seconds. Then start over and do the circuit one more time to complete a total of 10 minutes.

NOTE - *The bottom line is that any workout is better than no workout. Start building short workouts into your day and soon you will feel stronger, leaner, and more energized.*

№ 3

*Calmness of mind is one of the
beautiful jewels of wisdom.*

-James Allen

Attention Span & Focus

5 RULES

1. STOP MULTITASKING
2. EXERCISE
3. **MEDITATE**
4. MOTHER NATURE
5. REDUCE INTERFERENCE

LEARN INNER, SMILE MEDITATION

By smiling inwardly to our organs and glands, the whole body feels loved and appreciated. The body's stress and tension invariably dissolve as smiling gets the nervous system to induce the relaxation response in our body.

1. Sit in your normal meditation posture and close eyes.

2. Relax your face, loosen your jaw muscles, cheeks, chin, lips and eyes. Feel them becoming calm and more relaxed.

3. Turn the corners of your mouth upward in a slow gentle smile.

4. Focus on the feeling inside as you start smiling. This will move attention away from any troubling thoughts.

5. With your eyes still closed, 'see' the eyes smiling too. Next move your awareness to the cheeks, chin and lips.

SIGNS OF PROGRESS IN MEDITATION

- *You feel more motivated*
- *You are sleeping better*
- *You stop keeping track of how long you meditate.*
- *You are less stressed*
- *You have more room in your mind*
- *You start to look forward to it*

Principle
№3

I go to nature to be soothed, healed and have my senses put in order.

-John Burroughs

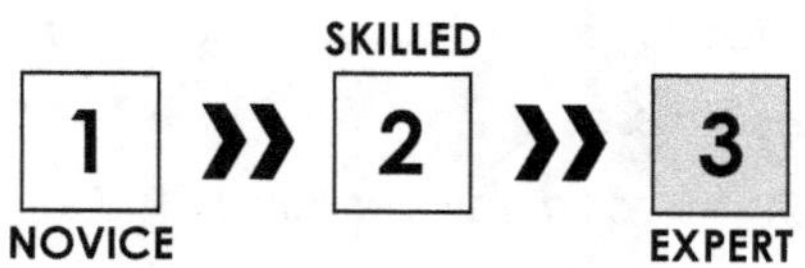

Attention Span & Focus

5 RULES

1. STOP MULTITASKING
2. EXERCISE
3. MEDITATE
4. **MOTHER NATURE**
5. REDUCE INTERFERENCE

📝 ASK AWARENESS QUESTIONS

Whenever you go outside, one of the easiest ways to enhance the experience for yourself or others is simply by asking questions that expand awareness. Ask the questions listed below as you're out in nature and write down the answers.

- What are you noticing right now?

  ....

- Have you ever seen this plant?

  ....

- What are you hearing?

  ....

- Do you hear that bird call?

  ....

- Do you smell those flowers?

  ....

NOTE - *The purpose of asking questions is not to have a direct answer. It's about opening awareness and helping you experience more. Each time you ask a question, it causes a shift in your perspective.*

There are always distractions, if you allow them.

-Tony La Russa

SKILLED

1 » 2 » 3

NOVICE   EXPERT

Attention Span & Focus

5 RULES

1. STOP MULTITASKING
2. EXERCISE
3. MEDITATE
4. MOTHER NATURE
5. REDUCE INTERFERENCE

📝 BE AWARE WHEN YOUR MIND LOSES FOCUS

Understanding the types of thoughts that distract you from work can help you avoid thinking about them in the future. Become aware of what thoughts are key distractions and then re-center your mind on what you are working on.

- What are two common distractions that come up often during work?

  1 ....

  2 ....

- What can you do ahead of time to prevent those distractions from happening?

  ....

  ....

- Write down a word you can say to yourself when you feel your mind getting distracted. This is the word you'll say when you need to re-center and get back to work.

  ....

NOTE - *Declining focus could result from lifestyle issues such as stress, fatigue, poor sleep, dehydration, unhealthy diet or sedentary behavior.*

Principle
№ 1

Sitting for even five minutes with a journal offers a rare cease-fire in the battle of daily life.

-Alexandra Johnson

Journaling

 **THE BEST COMPLIMENT**

What was the nicest thing anyone has ever said to you? How did it make you feel and how did that moment play out? Journaling is a great way to revisit a happy memory after a long day, so try this mental health prompt the next time you're having a bad day.

NOTE - *Use the free space above to sketch and doodle all the random thoughts in your head. It will help you concentrate and spur creative insight.*

FREEDOM SPACE

Journaling *continued*

FREEDOM SPACE

FREEDOM SPACE

■■ FREEDOM SPACE

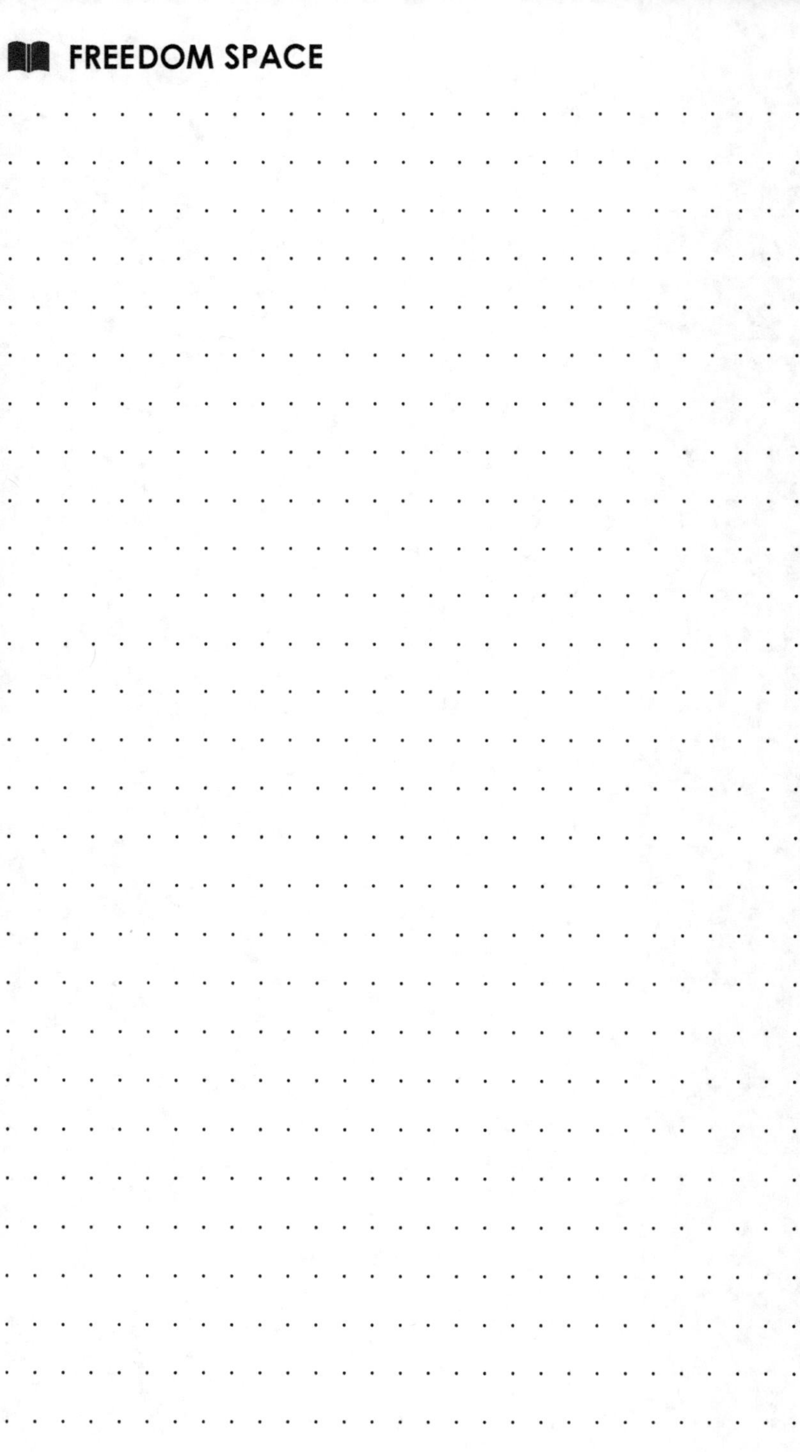

FREEDOM SPACE

FREEDOM SPACE